Activate your Home or Office

For Success in

Growth and Wisdom

With Feng Shui

Copyright © 2016 Termina Feng Shui. All rights reserved. No part of this book may be reproduced or transmitted in any form without written permission from the authors and publisher, except for brief inclusion of quotations or for review purposes. First Edition

This book is designed to provide competent and reliable information regarding the subject matter covered. However, it is sold with the understanding that the author and publisher are not engaged in rendering legal, financial, or other professional advice. Laws vary from country to country and if legal or other assistance is required, the services of a professional should be sought. The intent of the author is only to offer information of a general nature to help you in your quest for well-being, the author and the publisher assume no responsibility for your actions. The author shall have no liability or responsibility to any person or entity regarding physical, psychological, emotional, financial, commercial damages, special, incidental, or consequential by the information contained in this book.

Contents

Introduction
What is Feng Shui
Invite your desired growth in
Clutter management
Activate your Growth and Wisdom
- Personal Growth and Development
- Meditation
- Family Collaboration
- Relationships with Children and Grandchildren
- Motherhood and Compassion
- Empowerment/Self-Empowerment
- General Supportive Luck
- The Trinity of Luck
- General Collaboration
- Enhance Your Connection to Heaven
- Business Collaboration
- Education Collaboration

Growth and Wisdom enhancers
- CLARITY
- CELEBRATION
- HONESTY and HONOUR
- PURITY
- JOY
- TRANSPARENCY
- FAITH
- TRANSFORMATION
- TENDERNESS
- HARMONY and BALANCE
- FOCUS

General and quick tips
- Dining Room
- Bedroom
- Bathroom
- Front Door
- Cleansing
- General

Create a vision Board

The power of You

Introduction

If we were to ask others; what is the foremost area of life that needs attention? Many would respond with good health. After all, without good health many areas in our life do not function well. However, there is an area that requires our purposeful attention, more than we sometimes realise. Without it we cannot improve our health or others areas of our life.

Wisdom and Growth is this area. This is how we became who we are, how we learned to pick up an object, walk, talk and function through life. This area requires our attention in addition to other areas for us to have a better experience in life. For example, if you have poor health or wealth, this may not be because of lack in those areas, but rather a shortfall in your skills or knowing what is required to improve your life to better. Feng Shui principles for wisdom and growth open the flow of Qi for the experiences and happiness you desire in your life, as well as getting to know yourself.

The important thing to remember is that your environment is your physical visualisation board and this unconsciously creates your outcomes, 24 hours a day, 7 days a week. The Chinese and now quantum physics teach us that we are surrounded by energy, in fact, everything is energy. Our environment is energy. Einstein told us this *"Everything is energy and that's all there is to it. Match the frequency of the reality you want and you cannot help but get that reality. It can be no other way. This is not philosophy. This is physics."* Energy or energy forces in Feng Shui are termed as Qi (chi). A good flow energy, also known as frequency, leads to abundance, prosperity and happiness while negative energy leads to misfortune and unhappiness.

Whether you are Building, Designing, Buying, Renting, Selling, Living or Working in a premises, Feng Shui improves your life in so many ways. If there is something going on in your life that you wish to change or improve: Health, career, relationships, financial issues, support, business, wealth, or academic achievement. — You name it — it's all possible by adjusting your environment. All of life circumstances fall under the Feng Shui umbrella of possibilities and there is no limit to what you can improve or amplify positively when these ancient principles and science is applied.

With Feng Shui we can arrange our environment so that we receive maximum support with solutions for improvement, maximising the energy of the home or office for the occupants so that there is improvement in the health, wealth and relationship areas of their lives. The 4000 year old art and science of Feng Shui helps harness the power of good energy in the home and cures the effects of negative energy. Many home and business owners confirm to the fact that Feng Shui has helped them with their struggles and even result in a more attractive living or work space.

What is Feng Shui

Feng Shui is a science and ancient art based on laws that govern the flow of energy. The term Feng Shui translates to "wind-water" in English and is a Chinese Metaphysic Art, practised through formulas and calculations using energy forces referred to as Qi (chi). Both Feng and Shui are associated with good health and prosperity which is why the art is so highly regarded in the east. Energy in the environment remains stuck, people are prevented from moving forward, or experience unwanted circumstances, however, by increasing the flow of energy this clears the path to propel forward and to bring to fruition desired intentions. By creating Positive changes in the environment it produces improvements in the level and flow of Qi energy bringing high levels of good fortune and creating a more favourable and harmonious layout for a home or office.

Today Feng Shui is used widely around the world, seeing value in what the Chinese have known for years and the objectives vary depending on the home or business owners desired outcome. The common desired outcomes include; healthy family relationships, improved physical and mental health, preservation or growth of financial wealth and harmony. When we consider the energy, we put out and take in, and apply the Feng Shui principles, we discover that we have more control over our lives than we originally believed. Feng Shui is our opportunity to direct the flow of energy in our lives as we choose. For those of you looking for a way to bring more success into some or all areas of your life, you can use the basics of Feng Shui to help you achieve your goal.

This book contains tips provided in a manner through harnessing the positive energies that you and your property can receive through the use of Feng Shui principles.

Invite your desired growth in

Feng Shui is a science that works beyond the physical world of cause and effect, operating on an energetic level to bring you the highest levels of good fortune. Using Feng Shui principles you create a better flow of energy in your environment and consciously direct that flow to achieve the successes you desire in your life.

The positive energy of an environment surrounds you and influences you 24 hours a day, seven days a week, your whole lifetime, this also applies to uncured negative energy. Feng Shui is like a form of acupuncture or bar codes for the unified field of energy that includes your home and body. Activate or cure areas within your home or workspace and you start a flow of energy through your body, mind, and soul for more success in your career, health, relationships and growth.

Brain Waves - Your home or workspace is a living, vibrating energy in a vast unified field of energy. Everything in a home influences the flow of active and passive energy also known as positive or negative Qi. This energy wave of flow is similar to the brainwaves formed from your own thinking process. The outcomes in your life are results of brain waves you habitually create with your thoughts. And the outcomes you experience in life are either suppressed or enhanced by the energy fields or environmental brainwaves emitting in your physical surroundings.

There are two brainwave energy fields or environmental brainwaves are beta and alpha frequencies. Beta frequencies reflect chaos and are present in cluttered rooms, drab, dirty spaces, environments with no cosiness or spaces filled with depressing or violent images, dead flowers and piles of papers. This environment feels overwhelming and joyless. It produces victim mentality where one feels unsupported. It creates the feeling of struggling uphill. In this state it is very hard to create what you want toward a better life. However, when you begin to declutter and clean the spaces. Introduce colours and uplifting images, the beta energy wave's shift to bring in the flow of alpha brainwaves. You invite in new opportunities and attract more of the power available to you. This positive flow brings to you good fortune in your career, relationships, health and growth as well as feeling more empowered.

Feng Shui has shown through the centuries that improving your success in any aspect of your life is within your control. When you change or add other things such as colours or items or position yourself or your furniture, this creates a positive spiralling of energy upward that affects your good fortune and you are in a much better position to attract what you desire. When you decide what you want or to make a change in your life the first thing you must do is get rid of the old to make room for the new. If you want certain successes in your life, you must make room, change or add something to invite it in.

General Space Feng Shui is universal. Each of the eight compass directions, plus the center direction, is associated with a specific life area, element, number, shape, material, colour, and symbol. Some of the directions include a representative season and animal. Any area can be activated by placing specific elements, colours, items or images, in the specific compass direction and area of your home or workplace.

Compass directions for Growth and Wisdom, including Relationship with yourself are north for clarity and self-empowerment. South for balance and celebration. East for honesty, focus and collaboration. West for transparency, communication, creativity and joy. Northwest for, general supportive luck, transformation and faith. Northeast for harmony, general wisdom and growth. Southwest tenderness, general collaboration and compassion. Southeast for forgiveness and release.

If you look closely at your environment what is it telling you. Can you see the reflection of your results? Can you see what is or is not happening in your life by examining your home or workplace? Are there any objects or images that reflect a chaotic or busy life. Is there piles of washing in an area that never stops piling. Are there broken items or furniture displayed, or covered just to conceal the damage? Is there work around your home or workplace that you will get to one day? Or is your home an unbalance shape rather than rectangular or square.

Feng Shui teaches that our external environment will always reflect our internal environment. When we shift or change our outer environment this becomes an energetic shifter to the inner. When we align our physical environment with our aspirations this enables us to direct our lives, consciously change our experience and more importantly have command and choice with how we choose our life experiences to be.

However, before you activate your home or workspace you must understand the significance of love and appreciation of yourself, practice the energy of self-love. Create a new energy you need to manifest your intentions. Have faith, love and know that each of us are wonderful, any beliefs, fears or judgements are only influences from the environments we grew up in. Here is a quote from *Marianne Williamson, A Return to Love*, *"Our deepest fear is not that we are inadequate. Our deepest fear is that we are powerful beyond measure. It is our light, not our darkness that most frightens us. We ask ourselves, 'Who am I to be brilliant, gorgeous, talented, fabulous?' Actually, who are you not to be? You are a child of God. Your playing small does not serve the world. There is nothing enlightened about shrinking so that other people won't feel insecure around you. We are all meant to shine, as children do. We were born to make manifest the glory of God that is within us. It's not just in some of us; it's in everyone. And as we let our own light shine, we unconsciously give other people permission to do the same. As we are liberated from our own fear, our presence automatically liberates others."*

- Be sure to create spaces that reflects what you desire. Only allow objects and images you love and remove anything you do not love. Surround yourself with images of people who give you loving support and encourage you to be yourself. Love and appreciate yourself.

Clutter management

Letting go of the past is Forgiveness as is letting go of things that have negative connections or serve no worthwhile purpose. This makes space for positive replacements. Feng Shui recognises that clutter can make people feel disorganised, uncreative, tired, anxious and burdened. Energy or Qi is all around us, all the time, the clutter is a clutter of energies.

Positive Qi, can become blocked by clutter. When energy is blocked, it becomes stagnate and then turns to negative energy. That is why one of the main principles of Feng Shui is that you must de-clutter your home. It's important to remember that getting rid of the old makes way for the new.

Start by clearing out everything that doesn't need to be there, unload it. In order to get new things in your life you have to release old things. Look around your home. Let go of Failure. If you have relationship problems, let go of things, letters, postcards, cards, pictures and items that are representing lack of harmony in relationships. If you have financial problems, let go of things, papers, files, pictures and items that are representing lack of financial abundance. Let go of anything representing your old business adventures, projects or jobs, that didn't work out for you, even study programs you never completed. Let go of everything representing your previous experiences that didn't work out for you. Put them all in a box and store it somewhere to tell the universe there is space for a renewed success. Release it all. If you do not have much time to clean and clear presently, place in closed spaces, or boxes and cover the boxes with beautiful fabrics. When clutter is visible, your sub conscious mind sends a message of chaos to the universe.

Sometimes it can be challenging to get rid of things that we don't need, but in doing so, we free up more of our energy to devote to the things we want. If you resist letting go of items because you spent money on them, then consider selling them. You can hold a garage sale, list them on Craigslist or eBay. If you still hold onto any items of ended experiences, then you are holding on to old energy patterns that block your Qi moving forward and your resistance is indicating lack and limitation, and you are not ready to move forward to your desired future. Even holding onto things for a later date, or just in case is indicating lack and limitation, as well as inviting some adversity to occur.

Here are some examples;

When we apply the best quality make-up this will not help the skin look healthy in the long term. If the skin is not cleansed and taken care of properly by using the correct procedures and products such as cleansers and good foods it will not stay vibrant and healthy. It also invites conditions to amplify unhealthy skin. When we hold on to the baggage from old relationships, they tend to carry over into new relationships, and this causes issues in the new relationship. If you were with someone for a period of time and they cheated on you, you may carry the belief that you have been burnt in this way, so you have built up resistance to complete trust and faith. This can spill over to your new partner and, even if they are not cheating, sometimes you feel there may be something they are not telling you. And it causes a fight until eventually you break up. It's the same concept with clutter in your home. If you carry all that old clutter around, there is no room in your life for new things to prosper. Abundance will pass you by because you're too busy holding on to lack and clutter.

Your living areas
Represent the present. Too much clutter creates stagnant Qi as well as inconvenience and frustration. Remove items that are from previous ailments or items given to you that you do not particularly like. Place something that makes you feel good and

makes you smile. Lilac represents the frequency of releasing, use lavender oils in your soaps, lotions and cleaning products to cleanse the stagnant, dense Qi.

Outside areas

Represents the present. Clear gardens of dried plants, or rubbish lying around, clean paths and maintain this, it allows the flow of positive Qi to enter. No faded, broken items or dried plants, the positive Qi is not present in these.

The Basement or under your home/office

Represents the past. This is better place to store things, however, too much stored indicates you are trapped in the past.

The attic

Represents the future. Too much stored here can block your future and the futures of generations to come. Avoid storage above the bedrooms or lounge room.

Improve your Qi flow with FORGIVENSS and RELEASE

- Let go of possessions, emotions, and thoughts that keep you stuck, particularly of ended relationships.
- The colour violet represents forgiveness
- Elevate the level of Qi in your environment and yourself.

Activate your Home or Office For in Growth and Wisdom

- Let go of photos, objects, and furnishings from your past that no longer serve you
- Reliving old memories is stagnant Qi. Let go of the past, things that have no allocated space or serve no worthwhile purpose. Remember that getting rid of the old makes way for the new Qi. Move on to make new, happy memories. Free up the stuck, dense energy to create a brilliant future
- Have a more positive outlook and focus on the things you are grateful for. Start a gratitude journal. Each day write three things you are grateful for.
- Antiques can have mental, emotional, and even spiritual impressions attached to them, release the dense Qi of the past by using lavender, geranium, and rosemary essential oils added to water for cleaning.
- Clear and organise your home or workspace to get the energy flowing, and prepare for new people, experiences, and opportunities into your life. Create space for good fortune to enter your life by creating an uncluttered space in every room.

Activate your Growth and Wisdom

A Feng Shui consultant uses the combination of Space Feng Shui and Time Feng Shui.

Space Feng Shui assessments determine the directions Qi flows in and around your physical environment. This includes General space orientation and activation of the home or office as well as activating and enhancing Personal Space Feng Shui based on an individual's Personal fortune directions to improve/increase Success, Health, Relationships and Growth. Time Feng Shui is the analysis of time cycles or Visiting Energy Assessments and the nature of specific energy flows of time cycles. All have their appointed compass direction, each of these nine directions have significant purposes, and the northeast corner of your home or workplace is your general wisdom and growth sector.

Personal fortune directions or Personal Space Feng Shui as mentioned above can only be assessed on an individual basis where a person's birthdate and other factors are required for accurate assessment. General Space Feng Shui is universal, the following pages contain general space wisdom and growth to self-practices.

Feng Shui and quantum physics teaches that everything in our physical environment carries an energy that is moving our lives forward in that direction. By placing in our physical surroundings objects or images that have a positive personal meaning, we are activating and sending the Qi in this direction every time we look at it. Even if we think we do not see it any longer, it is still registering the message on a sub-conscious level.

Personal Growth and Development

The self cultivation, education and knowledge direction of the Northeast represents your personal growth and development. It opens great wisdom about yourself and others, providing greater insights, and inspiration. This area is where you explore who you are authentically by exploring your thoughts and feelings about what you really want that brings you long-lasting joy.

You can activate and use this area of your home or workplace as a place to expand your spiritual nature, feel inspired, create more time, study, learn, retain and remember easily, as well as bring examination luck, scholastic honours, scholarships and literary success. You can even have others resonate with your ideas or listen to your wisdom. It is also the place where you can retreat to when you need to switch off and recharge, a place to read and develop your inner wisdom. Enjoy the special energy of the space by practicing Qigong, yoga, prayer and meditation. It supports all types of educational pursuits that can improve your life, add to your intuitive abilities and support your understanding of your core desires.

When improvements are made to this direction of your surroundings in combination with improvements made to the complementing areas, you can positively impact what you know and gain insights in what you can do. Start by decluttering and cleaning this direction. Place some drops of lavender oil in your cleaning products. This detoxifies dense negative Qi. As stated in the previous chapter clutter clearing is essential for creating a positive flow of Qi. All activations including colours, objects or plants will negate against the low, depressing energy of clutter. Unclutter your spaces, cupboards and drawers, available space invites free flowing Qi. Clutter constantly drains energy from you. Open, clean, clear and organised space welcomes new opportunities and invites room for your growth to improve, flourish and thrive.

Objects can have mental, emotional, and even spiritual impressions attached to them, as well as a space. Place a little sea salt and rice in the northeast direction and leave it there for an entire day, if this area does not feel peaceful, place a bowl of water with sea salt there for seven days.

Quality of air

We are fed by the air we breathe and the impact of our surroundings. The environment is influenced by the level of Qi in a room, breathing clean air keeps your own energy open. Fresh, good quality air is often ignored, and this is a Feng shui priority. Aerate your spaces to bring in new fresh Qi and replace recycled air. Ensure you maintain high levels of Qi by opening windows and doors wide and often, do whatever it takes to find solutions for better air in your home. An oil burner, incense, ioniser or air purifier will enhance the positive flow. Ensure the air you breathe is clean.

Natural light

This also includes indoor lighting. Once you focus on the quality of light in your environment you will feel a positive shift in your health and well-being. Light as well as colour are our nutrients, particularly sunlight. Give your environment and body enough light nutrition. If any spaces are limited with natural light ensure that you use lamps in the dark areas. All the four corners of each room in your home or workspace should be well-lit. Dark areas and corners create dense, negative Qi. If you are unable to light all four corners of each space, ensure that every corner of your living room has light. If you have fluorescent light bulbs, replace them if possible, they increase electromagnetic energy that interferes with health use LED lights or lamps instead of the general lighting if these are fittings in your home. Also place in your home or workspace vibrant art, ensure it is happy and joyful with fresh, alive colours. Be it a wall colour, art or fresh flowers, your energy is strengthened by the presence of colour and light.

The Northeast direction is enhanced when it is peaceful and quiet. It works well as a library, study area, meditation or relaxation space. This direction is not just for students who are in school or for someone who wants to further their education. This direction also applies to life skills and better understanding through knowledge. For example; Are you struggling with your finances and want to learn to manage them better or ways to increase it? Are you interested in learning a new language? Want to change your career yet have no experience or skills to attain something more rewarding? Are you looking to have a better spiritual understanding of the world or want to have a deeper understanding about yourself?

Decluttering and cleaning is the start in creating a flow of positive Qi. By placing items and images you activate environmental affirmations that represent what it is you want to have happen in this area of your life. These environmental affirmations are your physical visualisation board. Every time you look at your items or objects you are sending the Qi in this direction, consciously and unconsciously. Activate in the northeast, a calm area of your home and workplace. Also in the lounge room for intuition.

Before activating ensure you establish what it is that you want. Below is a brief list that can help you along the way;
- Want to move forward and release past and/or present issues.
- Interested in starting a spiritual practice such as meditation
- Feel the need to slow down and spend more time on self-reflection
- Desire to get out in nature more and connect to the wisdom of the universe
- Want to start a new path of learning

- Want to start a new career or finally have a career
- Want to create an atmosphere to focus and study
- Starting a new job that requires using new skills
- Want to retain and recall quickly any information
- interested in cultivating a more peaceful mind and/or lifestyle
- Just want to feel less stressed and more relaxed
- Interested in developing your spiritual path

Place items or images in this area of your home or workspace that remind you of the things you want to learn, understand and improve upon. Use reference materials, reminders of self-improvement goals, poems, affirmations that support your happiness, school work, projects and books that symbolise your current skills that you would like to master or skills you would like to learn. Some examples are: books on being happy, mastering your finances, meditation practices, success principles or healthy lifestyles, as well as books by spiritual and success mentors. Add a metal bell, this indicates clear as a bell. If you read newspapers daily, do not leave them here when you are done or for long periods of time. Newspapers contain many negative articles this can cause information to be overloaded.

Also place items that support your quiet time for self-reflection, meditation or prayer, such as; Images of quiet places in nature, still mountain pictures, quotes and inspirational sayings. Art with earthy tones, the northeast is represented by the earth element.

Remember you are growing every day in learning about your business or personal goals so this is the place for reminders of anything that improves your productivity. Display personal recognition items that remind you of your achievements. Awards, certificates or trophies.

Ensure there is space for an altar or something similar in the northeast direction. It can be a bench, cushion or whatever you choose. This is where you express who you are, make a deep connection by feeling the gratitude for what you've been blessed with, and ask for guidance and protection. There are many deities, traditional or cultural that represent heavenly blessings. Place an image or statue on your altar such as Mother Mary, Isis, Kuan Yin, Jesus, saints, angels, the laughing Buddha or wise people. Your connection to the divine power within is a very intimate connection, ensure you choose only those that deeply and truly connect to you. Also place a red, orange or purple tall candle, objects of inspiration and personal meaning such as things you found in nature, crystals and items that are shaped as squares, this strengthens the area. Spend some time sitting in front of your altar, completely clearing your mind and focusing just on your breath.

Your Personal Fortune Directions and Time Feng Shui for Wisdom and Growth

Your Personal Fortune directions are based on your Kua number, and has a greater effect for you personally than general space Feng Shui. The areas include success, relationships, health and growth, and is established by gender, as well as date of birth. Money is associated with success, when you know your Personal Fortune Directions you can face it for added fortune, as well as place activations in these directions to amplify your personal successes. There are four misfortune directions as well. When you are aware of these directions you can cure and ensure specific placements are not hindering your successes. To establish the fortune colour, element, shape, fabric and other aspects for your growth requires a Personal Fortune direction analysis, a Feng Shui Consultant is recommended.

Never place anything into your space that you do not love just because you are told you to do so. Feng Shui is about creating a positive flow of Qi as well as creating a living space that feeds your soul and uplifts your spirits. Objects you don't love will have the opposite effect. The more personal the objects are to you, the more Qi they will generate. Representations of items do not require to be only one thing such as Eastern symbols. An example is the Chinese symbolism for a tortoise, the Celestial Guardian of the North, this can be represented by any tortoise, live, image or object.

Meditation
There is greater productivity after a time-out. We must have moment of calm at the end of a cycle and before the beginning of a new one. Nature shows this very clearly through the stillness of winter, to prepare for the activity of spring. We live in an active world with technology, attitudes, daily tasks and general living. Meditation is the key way to relax as well as fill your mind and body with positive energy. Meditation also gives you an opportunity to create your desired future.

Getting to know ourselves is one of the greatest occupations we can volunteer to ourselves. We can pursue things many times in life, believing this one or that one is going to make us happy, and when we receive it we are not as happy as we thought we would be, or the novelty of it washes away within days, weeks or months. How satisfied we are with the decisions we make is a measure of how well we know ourselves. When we give ourselves quiet time to get in touch with ourselves and meditate, we gain clarity and insight into what we truly want. These true self desires are the ones that make as happy with lasting results.

Meditation is Self-Knowledge Practice and true security lies in our connection to the source within. When your true identity is known and experienced, the present problems weaken and do not bother you for too long. Meditation positively influences your health, as well as production for happy and successful future events of your life. It amplifies clarity and serenity, this gives opportunity to plan in the physical life successes, pleasures and invites more like energy to keep flowing into your experience. Meditation is the place where you can hear the answer of your own heart. This helps to plan your desires for love, happiness and prosperity.

There are many ways you can meditate. You can listen to a guided meditation, place soft, calming music on, or have a completely quiet space. Start your meditation with fresh breaths of inhaling and exhaling. Ensure that your arms or legs are not crossed. Inhale through your nose, hold for a few seconds then exhale out of your mouth. Just focus on your breathing and this will begin the process of your relaxed state. Just allow yourself to wander deeper into this relaxed state and allow whatever comes to mind flow naturally.

Create a meditation room or area where you can light a candle, put on calming sounds of nature, add essential oils, such as sandalwood, sage and frankincense and just breathe. There are many things in life that are achieved through activity, however, wisdom is one that comes to us when we stop activity, reflect upon our experiences, connect to ourselves and to our Creator. We must give ourselves time to rest, recover and recharge our batteries. Place items, images or books in the northeast such as meditation books, a singing bowl or meditation tools, if you want to learn, understand and improve upon meditation.

Family Relationships

To have a family that is loving and supportive at all times is a blessing. To have a healthy, beautiful and happy environment to share with your family is to be blessed twice. Good family, friend and work relationships enhances personal growth.

The art and science of Feng Shui is intricate and complex. Houses and their surroundings are studied carefully for their influence on people living in the house. The quality of energy in your home determines the quality of your everyday family interactions and when Feng Shui principles are implemented, this creates positive energy flow in the environment for all household members, both young and old. Feng Shui practices invite better relationships with your children or your family and will help you bring more peace and understanding into your family life.

Areas of your home represents a specific area of your life:

The Centre

The center of your home is considered very important, because it is from the center that all other areas of your home draw their energy nourishment. The center is called the heart of the home, or the yin yang point. The more open and happy the center of the home is, the happier and more open the people who live in that home tend to be. Take good care of your center by creating vibrant and harmonious energy there, place happy items and images, what happiness means to you and your family.

Lounge/Family Room

The energy of family harmony is closely connected to the family bagua area of your home. Place in this area elements of vibrant wood, a fountain for positive Qi flow, clear or rose quartz crystals as well as happy family photos.

Express Happiness

Quantum physics states like attracts like energy. A home that is clean, clutter free and loved will attract and promote harmonious communication between all family members. Organise your home so that everything has its place. Most importantly, express love and care with all your home contents, this indicates good support, care, happiness and well-being of your family. Create a home that is beautiful, joyful and full of love.

Family Collaboration

For better collaboration between family members and friends, place a picture of the entire family, or members of the family with whom you would like to collaborate in the East direction in lounge/family room, which is the general direction for family. The East is connected with a forest that represents a family of trees and wildlife, place a family tree here. If you work with family, activate collaboration in the East direction of your workplace as well. Avoid placing wastebaskets or clutter here. The lounge/family room is considered the area where the family comes together. How the space is organised can help the whole family live together in harmony:

Compassion

Southwest stands for compassion. Create a gentle ease of love and support in the way you relate to yourself and others. *"Be gentle first with yourself if you wish to be gentle with others." ~Lama Yeshe.*

When we feel compassion for others, we feel kindness toward them, empathy, and a desire to help. It's the same when you are compassionate toward yourself. Self-compassion creates a caring space within you that is free of judgment. An important part of living a happy and fulfilling life includes being part of sharing, helping and supporting people you care about. It also includes being kind to strangers, and learning to replace envy and anger with understanding and empathy. Allow yourself to see that *everything* around you is sacred.

Enhance compassion in this direction of your lounge room or bedroom by placing an image or statue of your 'Mother of Compassion': Kuan Yin, Mother Mary, Tara, Mother Theresa, Isis or someone who represents compassion to you.

-Feel more compassion for yourself, others, and for the world you live in

- Go easy on yourself when you try new things or make mistakes

- Show trust in others and treat them with patience and gentleness

- Have patience to listen to your inner voice and the advice of others
- Be more open to others

Empowerment/Self-Empowerment

Manifest Your Power by being open to transform your life. When you start to change things, make the changes with the right attitude. Proceed fearlessly. Do not complain about the changes you need to make or it will block the ease of making them. Look for support available to you and believe you will have all the help you need. Let go of things and situations with joy. When something does not serve you anymore, be thankful for what you received from it. Recycle it to bless someone else. Place ornaments and move furniture with a sense of blessing. In between every change, take time to experience the impact and enjoy the process.

--Forgive yourself and release the past. Write a list of what you forgive yourself for or say it out aloud.

-Have courage to make necessary changes

-Create collaboration with all of the support available to you

-Love yourself and release judgment. Hold the intention that it will empower you to do your Feng Shui decluttering, cleaning, and activations now.

- Be more outgoing

- Learn how and when to say no. This is a crucial step towards reclaiming your personal sense of empowerment. You control your own choices.

General Supportive Luck

Have more friends, enhance your general supportive luck and friendships, mentoring relationships, your relationship with your father, and relationships with your children by placing Items or images in the northwest of your Home, Office or Yard, such as Images of supportive kinds of relationships: fatherhood, personal pictures with your father, mentors, friendships, or an image of helping hands. Do no place the Fire elements such as a candle. No wastebaskets, clutter, or yard waste in these corners because the accumulation creates density and slows the flow of positive Qi.

When you work in business with your friends, father, or children, enhance the Northwest area in your workplace as well.

The TRINITY of LUCK

In Feng Shui, there are three categories which describe the type of luck we experience in our lives, they are:

Heaven Luck- This refers to the karma, destiny, health types, astrological horoscope and the family environment you were born into and is determined by the cycles of time. This type of luck cannot be controlled. You can however, through astrological cycles or the Chinese Astrology Almanac, also known as the Tung Shu prepare for times when you are more likely to experience positive and negative points towards key areas in your life such as health, relationships, career, or finances. It helps to take note of astrological periods. This indicates where your key life lessons will be more likely to occur. Your astrological chart also helps determine areas where you are more likely to experience luck potential. These astrological events can affect communications, contractual problems, delays, travel, machinery breakdown and times of change and unexpected news. To make the most of your overall luck potential, you should develop a positive, progressive attitude while applying Feng Shui principles to your home and work environment, as well as keeping up to date with major astrological changes in your life. Luck is ultimately when skill and knowledge, plus the right attitude, meet opportunity. Feng Shui can help the flow of Qi that attracts positive energy, this increases your abundance opportunities.

Earth Luck - This type of luck is determined by our surroundings for example our home or workspace and the way in which we direct ourselves with positive or negative energy combinations, within and around the earth. This type of luck can be improved and enhanced when Feng Shui is correctly applied to your home or work environment. It deals with balance, element cycles, mathematical probability factors, magnetic orientation, surrounding landform and time dimensional analysis.

Human Luck - This refers to your personal attitude, education, managerial and financial ability, lifestyle, virtues, the choices that you make and your personal quest for knowledge. As an individual, you have full control over this type of luck, and when it is combined with Earth Luck through the correct application of Feng Shui, you increase your experience for greater harmony, contentment and success. To truly experience the joys which life can offer, you must first examine your attitude and sense of self. Change your attitude and you can quite literally change your life. You can utilise positive symbols, words and images within your surroundings to help focus and connect your personal aspirations with the appropriate Earth Luck location combinations.

- Learn to recognise your negative self talk. We all do it to some extent. Change it to an uplifting phrase.

- The positive and negative behaviours in your life have had many years to shape you into the unique individual that you have now become. Learn to look at yourself objectively in order to recognise certain conditioned responses and patterned behaviour, this can be enlightening.

- Acknowledge each positive step that you take forward.

- Surround yourself with positive friends and family who will encourage and support you.

- Actively seek to learn and experience as much as you can from the people and environment around you. Learn from someone who has what you want. Knowledge is life with wings. Find yourself a mentor someone who you aspire to be like and admire for what they have achieved in their life. Observe the ways in which they conduct themselves.

- If you find yourself feeling negative resolve it through forgiveness. You may not alter a situation immediately, but you can take full control of your response to the situation and how you ultimately deal with it.

General Collaboration

Improving collaboration amplifies your efforts. Remove any symbols that contradict collaboration such as: images of yourself alone; images of animals attacking, battles, or other tragedies, images of people or animals facing away from each other. Activating relationship directions of your workplace improves your professional collaboration and activating the relationship direction in your lounge room or bedroom will improve your spiritual collaboration. To increase collaboration, place the pictures or items for your activations together so they give a feeling of togetherness. Put these pictures in a fuchsia frame

-Learn from others, there are gems in all we experience

- Share the workload. This will invite a positive flow of Qi for all.

- Share a common sense of accomplishment. Be happy for another's success, when you rejoice for another your rewards increase.

Enhance Your Connection to Heaven

The direction connected to the Northwest is called Helpful People and Blessings or Connection to Heaven and help from Heaven, it also relates to patriarch and patronage luck representing the full force of Yang energy. This direction within the home or workspace aligns your connection with the outside world including your mentors, work colleagues, friends, networking, benefactors and business prospects.

Place an activation here for the energy to help attract beneficial people in your life. We all need somebody to help us. We all need a mentor. Mentors do not only refer to people who are in power who can teach us things or help us in achieving our goals, this also refers to people who may not be our senior in stature, age, experience, but are around us can is able to contribute to our success. Place silver bells and a singing bowl in this direction. Avoid water images as they will deplete the favourable energy.

In Feng Shui, by activating our Mentor's Luck we start to attract people who help us along the way. Begin by being positive yourself this starts the flow of a powerful positive aura, which in turn will attract people who are also positive.

This direction also supports the energy of travel, if you would like to travel more, express this energy here. Travel is also beneficial to health, new environments equals a new flow of Qi. Place travel photos, and maps. Photos of people who have helped you grow in life are also good to display or spiritual mentors, symbols, teachers, and angels that support us. Do not put a fire element, candles in the Northwest of home, lounge room, or other important rooms because it symbolizes fire at heaven's gate. If you have a fireplace in the Northwest, place a bowl of still water next to it, the water element represents diminishing the fire energy.

Business Collaboration

Enhance relationships with your business or work colleagues.

For better collaboration with your manager, supervisor, mentor, personal coach, or boss, activate the northwest direction in your workplace, it stands for hierarchy and is connected with heaven, the father, the stars, and the planets. Place a picture of you and your intended collaborator along with their business card attached to yours. If you want help from powerful and influential people, this is the sector to activate. Display a wealth ship (with sails, no cannon holes) here and pile up with coins, jewellery or gemstones.

For better collaboration with your work colleagues or business partners, activate the Southwest direction in your workplace. This direction represents general collaboration. Place a team picture or a ceramic circle of animals or people.

If you are in business with your romantic partner, mother, or children, also activate the Southwest in your workplace with personal pictures on display.

When working with others in your office, add a round table, this shape enhances collaboration and a mastermind of problem solving ideas.

Arrange the surface of your desk with Feng Shui principles. The nine directions or bagua is a map that can be applied to your desktop as well as your computer, just as it would be applied to the floor plan of a home or office. Different areas of the bagua are associated with different areas of your life, for growth and wisdom place as follows:

- The front left corner of the desk is associated with wisdom. Place the colour blue here, as well as symbols of things you'd like to learn, can help you acquire more knowledge and that can help you in your career.

- The front right corner represents helpers and travel. Place the colour grey here, as well as contact information, such as an address book, your phone, or a travel guide or photo of a vacation spot.

- The right side center of the desk represents your creativity and focus. To boost this place the colours silver, gold, white, and copper also add inspirational materials, such as quotes or books. For the computer place icons such as put your spiritual files, agenda, and important personal papers in a folder in the northeast of the screen which is the bottom left hand corner of the computer screen to enhance your growth and wisdom flow. For Personal fortune growth and wisdom, this can be established through a Personal Feng Shui analysis by a Feng Shui consultant.

For those who have a home office or work from home, you can apply the same Feng Shui principles as in any other work environment. Keep the entrance of your home neat, clean, and free of clutter, including the entrance to your office space. Even if clients do not attend this workplace this is essential in opening the flow of energy and welcoming positive improvements to your work life.

Education Collaboration

For a student who would like to have a great collaboration with their teacher activate collaborative help with your studies or work. Place books, study material or work related paper work in the northeast direction.

The type of teacher desire to collaborate with will determine which area you will activate. Activate your workplace or study area for a teacher of knowledge and skills, such as your business mentor or personal coach. For a teacher of spiritual wisdom, activate your living room and bedroom by placing an image of you with your teacher, a book or material done by your teacher.

Your Personal Fortune Directions and Time Feng Shui for Money and Success

Your Personal Fortune directions are based on your Kua number, and has a greater effect for you personally than general space Feng Shui. The areas include success, relationships, health and growth, and is established by gender, as well as date of birth. When you know your Personal Fortune Directions you can face it for added success, as well as place activations in these directions to amplify your personal success. There are four misfortune directions as well. When you are aware of these directions you can cure and ensure specific placements are not hindering your success. To establish the fortune colour, element, shape, fabric and other aspects requires a Personal Fortune direction analysis, a Feng Shui Consultant is recommended.

Never place anything into your space that you do not love just because you are told you to do so. Feng Shui is about creating a positive flow of Qi as well as creating a living space that feeds your soul and uplifts your spirits. Objects you don't love will have the opposite effect. The more personal the objects are to you, the more Qi they will generate. Representations of items do not require to be only one thing such as Eastern symbols. An example is the Chinese symbolism for a tortoise, the Celestial

Guardian of the North, this can be represented by any tortoise, live, image or object.

Growth and Wisdom enhancers

Feng Shui cures obstacles, strengthens intentions and addresses how the Qi flows through an environment. A value of Feng Shui is to bring our awareness to those areas of our life which are not in harmony with our intention. There are several approaches to making these adjustments and enhancements by adjusting the home or workplace environment, even ourselves. We can remove negative Qi and other dense factors that distract, slow down or, in some other way, divert our intention for desired successes.

The Bagua directions of a home or workplace divides the structure or individual spaces into nine areas of life activity and these are connected by distinct energy fields of the spaces along with objects, images, plants animals and people. Through people and animals emotions and personal practises are also emitted. When you improve the energy of your home, you change yourself and your life and by applying the Feng Shui principles for self enhancement you evolve to fulfil your desires. Author *Napoleon Hill* explains, *"Our brains become magnetised with the dominating thoughts which we hold in our minds, and, by means with which no man is familiar, these 'magnets' attract to us the forces, the people, the circumstances of life which harmonise with the nature of our dominating thoughts."*

CLARITY

Clarity is the quality of being easily understood, expressed, remembered and of being easily seen or heard.

Feng Shui principles assist you in communicating more clearly by expressing your needs and desires openly, earnestly and wholly. Through establishing and applying your desires in your environment it creates impressive results from your efforts and avoids misunderstandings.

Clarity begins with deciding what you want. What type and level of knowledge or wisdom. How do you see growth? Prioritise areas where you require fast results. Determine exactly what you want to accomplish. Bring a clear, accurate message of your desired outcome for your growth, insights or inspiration. Place symbols, images or objects reflecting the outcome that you want to create. Let go of images that no longer clearly represent your intentions. Take care of what has not been completed now, just by starting and ticking off even your simplest tasks invites the positive Qi of clarity.

To send the best message about abundance and invite clarity, clean water features. Light up your home, workplace, yard and entry. Add bright objects and plants. Place happy items an images in the eight directions including the Centre of your home or workspace that represent growth.

Ensure the entrance and exterior to your home or workplace is well lit and has clear messages showing the world to recognise and respond to your personality or business as well as indicating that a very successful person is inside. Also Place happy items or images outside. Do not hang dark or depressing images.

CELEBRATION

South stands for fame and recognition as well as music, celebration, and festivity, activate the South area by placing orange objects in living room or workplace. Unless you want to get pregnant do not activate celebration in the bedroom.

Celebrate your efforts and accomplishments, changes, significant dates and celebrate yourself! Cooked a great meal, celebrate, completed your tasks, celebrate, finished reading a book, celebrate. Add the positive flow of celebration to anything you choose to rejoice for.

Manifest more joy showing off your awards and place them in gold frames to invite abundance. This will give you more to celebrate.

Celebrate your accomplishments by throwing a party. Do not wait for others. Create celebrations for yourself. Feng Shui is a consistent celebration of positive flowing Qi. Include children in your parties, because they represent the fortune of the family.

HONESTY and HONOUR

Honour is connected to the east and power of the dragon, a symbol of power, truth, and magic. Place Dragon Symbol or object in your workspace or lounge room lower than eye level so it does not overpower you and enjoy the Dragon's precious cosmic breath.

Improve Human Luck: Feng Shui helps create an environment to change old habits, create more self-discipline and double your talents to their full potential. HONOUR is important, Eastern cultures practice Honour.

When the flow of life is good, ride the wave. When the flow of life is not great, check to see if it is keeping you from doing what you want to do. Contemplate your behaviour. Are your actions, thoughts and feelings honourable? If not what mental programs can you change and emotions can you release.

Keep structure and good life management, practice self-help/development. These are a strong indicators of how we can change our programs. Discipline yourself to fulfil your destiny and to fully express who you are. Make it easier to stick to your intentions and actions with your family and clients. Surround yourself with people who are truthful. Be more honest with yourself and others.

Improve Heavenly Luck: Practise spiritual lessons, Qigong, yoga, prayer, meditation and positive affirmations.

Improve Earth Luck: Your environment, home and workplace, is a greater body surrounding your physical body. Every object in your home or workplace is like a cell in the greater body. And as part of the unified field of the whole, will affect your body and physical experience. There are unseen links of energy between every material thing. All part of the Quantum Physics field. This can be improved with Feng Shui practices by allowing the positive flow of Qi.

For your workspace display a pair of Fu Dogs at the entrance door to protect you against office politics and corporate power struggles.

PURITY

There are 5 levels of purity: Physical Home, office and body, Etheric, Emotional, Mental and Spiritual.

Creating purity is essential if your thoughts and feelings are cluttered or chaotic, you are addicted to something or you feel abused or that people violate your boundaries.

Meditations, or exercises such as Qigong and yoga assist in creating stillness within the active mind. Visualise the light of the sun in your body and home with a light meditation. Open the windows and doors to bring in light and activate your senses. When natural light is low, use lamps in the dark areas. Ensure the four corners of each room in your home or workspace are well-lit. If you are unable to light all four corners of each space, ensure that every corner of your lounge room has light.

Clean your home or workspace with lavender oils mixed in with your cleaning products. Wash your physical body every day. Use lavender soaps or add lavender oil to your shower gel, lavender helps release toxins and old energies from your aura.

To invite purity into your body and new possibilities into your life, create space for what you want. Even the best activations are impeded upon in a cluttered or dirty environment, ensure you dust your furniture too.

Do not display broken objects. The life force or Qi in these objects are broken and gluing does not restore the Qi.

JOY

The West is the direction for Joy it also represents communication, and children's luck.

If you would like to appreciate everything your senses experience or you lack joy, feel sad or are depressed. Place fun, humorous items here. Add fabrics, colourful artwork, bright pillows or objects bright colours to lead eyes from colour to colour. Peach and orange are the best for joy, red and warm yellows add joy too. Activate in the lounge room for everyone to invite more joyful communication. Place joyful images, toys and smiling people. Allow more sunlight to enter the spaces and open windows to let the wind bring new Qi into the home. If you cannot open your windows, use air fresheners and burn candles. White and black colours do not create joy. Exposed beams in your entrance or lounge room can create sadness for everyone in the family, cover them in fabric or paint them the same colour as the ceiling.

TRANSPARENCY

Invite clearness of mind, body, emotions and environment. Ensure that your lounge room and workspace are clean and uncluttered. Become more organised and get your business or personal records in order

Etheric transparency

The etheric field is the energy body known as the first layer in the human energy field or commonly known as the aura. This field has less dense Qi than the Qi that surrounds the physical body. This energetic body or aura is fed by the air we breathe and the impact of our surroundings. Our etheric field is influenced by the level of Qi in a room. Low energy levels of Qi create negative thoughts and depressed feelings where high energy levels of Qi help us feel raised and happy. Ensure you maintain high levels of Qi by opening windows and doors. An oil burner, incense, ioniser or air purifier will enhance the positive flow. Ensure the air you breathe is clean. Be mindful of the images, objects, and paintings you display, this can create a negative impression on you.

Emotional transparency

Emotional fields from you and your family or past inhabitants may linger in your home or workplace. There may have been a break up or constant fighting. Place a little salt and rice in all of the corners of your spaces as a gesture of abundance and gratitude and remove it after one day. Also place water with sea salt in the centre of the home or workspace for seven days.

If you are experiencing arguments this may be associated with your kitchen. If your stove is opposite a sink this indicates disharmony, fire fights with water, water boils. Hang a pakua crystal between the stove and sink to unify fire and water. These are special 8-sided mirrors used to cure negative Qi. Door handles can also be associated with arguments if they hit against each other. Tie a red ribbon to the handles to symbolically establish unity between these arguing door handles then cut the ribbon evenly and tie them onto the handles.

Mental transparency:

Occasional sanctuary is required in our lives, particularly when you want to put ideas into action, slow down, restore clarity or when you want to be more relaxed mentally. For mental transparency create a room with less furniture, fewer books, fewer ornaments, and fewer things to tend. It can also be a chair and window focused on a view that is spacious or a bathtub filled with essential oils and natural suds. These are vital spaces to recharge our own energetic batteries, after all we are beings that contain electricity.

Also clean your desk when you finish working to be ready for fresh ideas. Keep alarm clocks at least five feet from your head when sleeping the electrical field disturbs your sleep and interfere with your focus.

FAITH

Have strong belief and trust in yourself as well as with the ancient art of Feng Shui. Create the new energy you need to manifest your intentions. Change the way you think, feel, and act. Apply the principles and invite your chosen positive destiny to unfold. Have patience with yourself and others. Recognise the results from your Feng Shui practices. Positive and negative responses can occur as you begin making changes. Respond in a positive way, and feel relief that there is finally a logical explanation for misfortunes in your life. Feng Shui changes can stir up energy and temporarily upset order, but it will calm down as the energy finds a new order. If you resist you lose focus and concentration. Resistance leads to fear and anger, have faith in your choices.

TRANSFORMATION

Have you ever thought, if only! Or if I could turn back time. Forgive and release the past, say goodbye to old behaviours and beliefs that no longer serve you, and say hello to a more positive incarnation of yourself, there always has and always will be time, life offers to many wonderful opportunities, you just have to invite them in and lay the groundwork for a better tomorrow to welcome your new success for what you truly desire.

Boost your learning, live a more conscious lifestyle, get the support you need to pursue your dreams. Change the way you feel in your surroundings, change your thought patterns or how you feel about yourself and recognise your transformations.

By applying these Feng Shui practices you have placed yourself in a transformation whirlwind, a waterfall of change. Some people feel overwhelmed and disoriented, which indicates that something is changing. Things must change to allow for the new to come. *Einstein's definition of insanity, "Insanity is doing the same thing over and over again and expecting different results.".* You are sane! Stay with it and look for the positive changes from your new energy flow!

Ask yourself, do I feel:

Happy and more confident that everything will be all right. Peaceful in my own home. Excited about my life and the changes I want to create. Comfortable in my space and no longer running away from it. A need to change many things in my life. A sense of accomplishment because I have made more changes in one week than I have in years. Able to handle things and climb out of a depression. Open to others and myself.

How has my thinking changed? Do I feel less fear, doubt, limitation, or loneliness? Do I express more power, self-esteem, and success?

Notice the changes in your personal growth. Peace or new people may have entered your life or an ideal book. You might begin a spiritual practice, find the teacher to help you reach enlightenment, become more devoted to your church, or do more volunteer work.

Notice other changes such as your activity level. You might complete little jobs around the house, spend more time playing with your children or associating with friends, take up painting or writing, or express your feelings better. People around you may be offering more encouragement to pursue your dreams, or help you find the right resources.

Start a positive flow journal. Observe and record positive changes in your life. Write gratitude statements. Write in your journal daily, use blue ink, this is the colour for power. Recording your positive flow will enhance a chain of positive change in your own experiences and empower others to become active in their own good fortune and luck.

TENDERNESS

Transform your bedroom into a place of nurturing sensuality and healing beauty, a place that has balanced energy. Be sure you genuinely love the way your bedroom looks and feels from wall colour and window treatment to your bed linens and bedroom art.

Create tenderness for yourself and your loved ones, find it easier to express appreciation and tenderness to your loved ones and be more open to receive tender attention from others. This is the most feminine or yin of all the bagua directions and is governed by the element Earth bringing essence of care, warmth, love and relationship. Place symbols of tenderness.

In your lounge room place a six-rod hollow metal wind chime. Wind chimes attract good chi. Ensure that it is a six-rod hollow metal wind chime. This wind chime is the best moving metal activator because it removes the density of the earth by attracting the energy of the earth in its hollow tubes. Change any angles or sharp edges of furniture, columns, shelves, pointed plants, ornaments, or objects to point away from where you and your loved ones sit. Hang crystals at large windows to reflect sunlight and create rainbows.

Feng Shui practice also means creating tenderness in the gifts you give your loved ones. Give personalised gifts with your heart. Place your gift in soft tissue paper. Do not give clocks or watches these symbolise that you do not have time for them or that time is running out.

BALANCE and HARMONY

Feng Shui is an art and science of principles derived from ancient Eastern practices that is designed to balance and harmonise the home or workplace which in turn creates balance and harmony within oneself. If one's home is healthy, then the individual can be healthy, in mind and body. This also assists with better insight to make the right decision, especially when you are torn between opposing situations, ideas, or people as well as help in resolving conflicts between people or to keep conflicts from escalating. When balance or yin and yang is achieved in the environment a positive energy flow is created.

There are many factors in an environment that can block this positive flow of energy, and one aspect is organisation.

Yin and yang are defined as two halves that together complete wholeness. When something is split or incomplete, it upsets the equilibrium of wholeness. This starts both halves chasing after each other as they seek a new balance with each other. Yang means "sunny or bright", and corresponds to the day and more active functions. Whereas yin, means "shady or dark", and corresponds to night and less active functions. These opposites are polarity required for harmonic balance. Opposing or contrary forces are complementary, interconnected, and interdependent in the natural world, and how they give rise to each other as they interrelate to one another. Duality exists in everything whether tangible or intangible, some examples are hot/cold, tall/short, or male/female. Duality is found in all and are parts of Oneness

Yang energy: white, heaven, male, active, day, sun, contraction, mountains, light colours, loud music, round shapes and round people, optimistic, energetic, young, outside and active.

Yin energy: black, earth, female, receptive, night, moon, expansion, valley, dark colours, silence or soft music, long shapes and tall people, pessimistic, exhausted, old, inside and passive.

When your life is out of balance, analyse the balance in your home and workplace. Balance the Five Elements: fire, water, wood, earth and metal. Also add air to the spaces. Each of these elements works independently and collectively to restore calm and bring energy to your space. Balance and harmony is imperative in Feng Shui practice, it is recommended that a Feng Shui Consultant is appointed to ensure this is created to its optimum level. However, below is a starter.

Earth – Earthy colour tones. Crystals or clay.
Metal – Silver or gold
Water – Blues. Water or glass.
Wood – Greens or browns. Timbers or plants.
Fire – Fiery colour tones. Sun or candles.

Create harmony for a stronger connection between who you are and what you do, to increase peace and harmony in your life as well as reduce the conflict, drama, and stress in your home or workplace. Create this in your landscape, home and workplace.

To do this the five elements – wood, fire, earth, metal, and water – must be in harmony in each room/space.

When an element is not represented in an area, place something of that element. For instance, missing the wood element, place something to represent wood. When an element is overpowering, weaken it with the appropriate element from the weakening cycle. For example, an overpowering timber room, place fire elements such as reds or candles in the space for balance. When one element creates a lot of chaos, clash, or disaster, repaint the room.

Use the elements listed below in various combinations, enhance, weaken, or control your spaces. Ensure all of the elements are represented in each space.

Productive Cycle:
WOOD fuels FIRE
FIRE creates EARTH
EARTH produces METAL
METAL condenses or holds WATER
WATER feeds WOOD

Weakening Cycle:
WOOD reduces WATER
WATER reduces METAL
METAL reduces EARTH
EARTH reduces FIRE
FIRE reduces WOOD

Destructive Cycle:
WOOD consumes EARTH
EARTH dams WATER
WATER extinguishes FIRE
FIRE melts METAL
METAL cuts WOOD

Wood harnesses the power of creativity and expansion. Wood also represents birth, strength, flexibility and intuition. There must be proper balance in the use of wood in your space as too much creates overwhelment, stubbornness and inflexibility. Not enough wood creates lack of creativity, indecision and depression. Place plants, paper, furniture or textiles. .

Fire increases enthusiasm and leadership skill. In the home fire is used to encourage expressiveness, inspiration and boldness. With fire a perfect balance is essential. Too much fire creates anger, aggression, irritability and impulsive behaviour. A lack of fire creates emotional coldness, lack of vision, inexpressiveness and low self-esteem. Place some candles, electronics or natural sunlight.

Earth affects our physical strength. It creates grounding, balance and stability. An overabundance of earth in a space, creates a sensation of boredom, sluggishness and seriousness. Too little earth creates disorganisation, chaos and lack of focus. Place images of landscapes or square shapes. Do not place images such as snowy mountains.

Metal affects mental clarity and logic. It creates organisation, focus, righteousness and analytical abilities. Too much metal creates chattiness, overly critical thoughts and speaking without thinking. Too little metal creates cautiousness and lack of focus. Place items of iron, aluminium, gold or silver.

Water responds to spirituality and emotion. A balance of water creates inspiration, wisdom and insightfulness. Too much creates feelings of unbalanced growth and the sense of emotionally drowning. It can make you feel overwhelmed and overly social. Too little water creates lack of sympathy, loneliness, isolation, and stress. Try incorporating water into your space by adding blacks, blues or reflective surfaces.

FOCUS

When focus is in balance you have fewer distractions and stronger concentration, stay focused on your goals, it improves your motivation for finishing projects you start and helps to recover from conditions or circumstances that diminish your focus.

To maintain focus decluttering all your spaces in the home, workplace and yard is imperative. Everything must have its place and there must be order. Even when items are in a cupboard or drawers, it must be easily accessible and not jammed full of things that fall out or must be removed to get to other layers.

A variety of influences such as architecture, furniture, plumbing, colours, shapes, objects, symbols, landscape, and surrounding environment can lead to an inability to focus. Below are features and factors in your home or workplace that can interfere with focus, and what can be done to activate greater focus right away.

Beams and Low Ceilings

When sleeping under a beam or a lower ceiling, people have problems with focus because these structures put pressure on their aura.

Beams that are straight across over the head symbolise the guillotine. Good energy will be cut off before it benefits you. Diagonal beams create distraction, good energy will start to flow but will not finish right. Beams that seem thin and sharp will have greater impact than beams that are flat and wide. Beams at an entrance influence the whole home. Sitting under beams for several hours has the same effect as sleeping under beams.

All beams and low ceilings above a bed and important areas must be cured. Move your furniture out from under any beam or lower ceiling. If your bed or seating area cannot be moved, cover the beam with fabric or paint the beam to match the ceiling. Fabric must not see through. Also create a canopy over the bed or seating area to block the pressure on your aura.

Street Traffic

Sleeping or working in a room where the street traffic faces you directly is a negative Feng Shui situation. The lights of the cars represent the eyes of the tiger stalking and attacking you. Ensure the widows have blinds or heavy curtains to block out the lights. Hang a pakua mirror on the outside of the window.

Bed Position

When bed is located on the same wall as the door, you cannot see the people coming into the room. Move bed. If moving the bed is not possible, hang a small mirror opposite the door so you can see anyone entering the bedroom. Do not sleep under a window. Moonlight on the head, brings trouble focusing during the daytime. If bed cannot be moved away from window. Place a heavy screen between your bed and the window.

For focus in the morning, remove electrical fields that interfere with focus during the night. Place alarm clocks at least 5 or 6 feet away from body unless they run on batteries.

Do not have a mirror reflecting the bed. A mirror that reflects your image when you are in bed scatters thoughts and create negative dreams. This applies to any reflective surface such as a television screen. Move all mirrors and reflective surfaces so you cannot see your image in bed or cover them before going to bed.

Bathrooms near bedrooms create focus problems. Keep the bathroom door closed day and night. Do not place bed against a bathroom wall. If your bed must be against a bathroom wall, place a mirror behind the headboard facing the bathroom to deflect the flushing of your energy field.

Poison Arrows

Any architectural features, furniture and pointed objects that aim toward you are considered poison arrows. For example, corners of tables, desks or any corner of two walls that are in line with where you work or sleep.

A poison arrow directed at your body as you work will interrupt your focus. If you notice poison arrows where you sit or sleep from cabinets or bookcases place fabric or an item to cover the arrow. Ensure that all books on shelves, even shelves with doors, are flush with the edge of the shelf. This prevents shelves from creating a horizontal cutting energy that disturbs focus.

General and quick tips

There can be many subtle factors in an environment that supports us with either positive or negative results in our growth success. Awareness and observation can move you from the negative to the positive flow.

Dining Room

Hang a mirror with a gold frame reflecting the dining table. This doubles abundance and the amount of people sharing a meal. Keep fresh fruit or flowers on the table. This brings life, energy.

Bedroom

The bedroom is for rest, rejuvenation and romance. Ensure your bed and bedroom support this.

Position the bed where the headboard is against a solid wall and that you can clearly see the entry door. Do not sleep under a window. Ensure your bed has balanced energy on both sides for example do not have one side of the bed up against a wall. Ensure both sides of the bed have a side table, light and a pleasant view.

Avoid family pictures in your bedroom, this is your private space and a place for you and your significant other. Family images here impede on your experience to fully enjoy your partner. If you have religious images or items, place them so that they are not directed at your bed.

Ensure items in the room have a proper place. There must also be order and unity to the room. Visual symmetry provides peace of mind, and it keeps the energy flowing through the room evenly.

Do not put water in the room, actual water or images with water, this attracts more unsettling dreams. No live plants or flowers because they have too much active yang energy for the bedroom calm yin energy is required.

Avoid work related items or exercise equipment. The bedroom is a passive space, not yang energy. Place your work desk or computer elsewhere. If you have no other place for a home office ensure the computer and all the work related items are put away before going to bed so you do not see it from your bed. The also applies to exercise equipment, place it elsewhere, not under the bed otherwise the active energy will promote a restless sleep.

Bathroom

Ensure that your bathroom is clean and organised and has a sense of beauty and pampering energy. Do not place photographs of friends or family members, as well as awards. These are drain areas, this tells the Universe you are flushing it all away.

To create tenderness in your bathroom ensure there is a pleasant smell, soft soap and bath linens, a closed toilet lid and bathroom door.

Front Door

Let go of failure. Remove anything representing your previous experiences that didn't work out for you. Look at the images hanging on the walls in your home, especially in your entrance, living room, bedroom and your workspace. Are they reminding you of something that is over? It's important that you do not place items or images of something that has ended at your entrance. Your entrance is the first impression of success when someone comes in to your home or workspace. Hang something more inspiring.

Start with your entry point also known as the mouth of Qi, and this includes your front door. It is the energy connection of your home. It is where the Qi enters along with what you and others bring or take with you.

Cleansing

Energy can neither be created nor destroyed; rather, it transforms from one form to another. When unpleasant feelings linger, space cleansing the environment transforms the energy to positive Qi leaving it lighter, healthier and happier, this creates more success. Everything that happens in an environment including conflict, trauma, and illness leave imprints and can attract other unwanted dense energy unless they are intentionally cleared. Subtle traces of past events can make places feel happy or sad. Replacing old carpet or furnishings, clutter management and redecorating all help to transform the negative dense Qi as well as cleaning the environment with lavender oils. Place a few drops of lavender oil in your cleaning products.

General

Add indoor plants and trees whenever you want growth. Avoid the cactus, as spikes invite criticism when grown inside. Try placing them in places where you spend or would like to spend positive time. The Qi or life-force of the plant, will energise the space as well as naturally removing indoor toxins and purify the air we breathe. Just remember that dead plants are a source of negative energy. If the plant is not blossoming, do not leave it sitting in your room to stagnate the flow you're trying to create. Add some motion to a space that is stuck. A stuck space usually reflects a stuck life. Move things around the room this helps liven the atmosphere. The Feng shui number to help guide you through this process of getting unstuck is twenty-seven. Just by moving twenty-seven things around a space whether it's a paper clip or a desk can bring positive energy to a room that was previously lacking it.

Welcoming, uplifting art should be hung in gathering spaces like a lounge room. Avoid solitary images in art in and out of the bedroom. Pictures of one person indicate the idea of being alone. Also avoid images such as storms, dead flowers and an uninhabited winter landscape.

Connect to your space personally to empower your life.

Display your trophies, favourite art or patterns you love this will help forge a strong bond between you and your environment.

In order to make a room look and feel magnificent, you must think about adding gravity and balance to the space. Think about your home or workspace as a living, breathing entity that wants to feel the same. A bare dining or coffee table with art on the walls feels very different to a table that has a centrepiece displayed. This centrepiece creates visual focus that organises the room in a new way, helping it to appear more settled.

Open space welcomes new opportunities and room to flourish and thrive. Clear space for happy conversations. By removing non-essential excess, it allows the flow for comfort and nestled joy.

Along with structure, items and colours your words create your environment, too. Something as subtle and innocent as a word enters our subconscious and affects how we feel. Be conscious on your vocabulary, and watch it shape your path. When we honour ourselves with good words, including praise for ourselves and others, we fuel our ability to live a good life.

Switch off the television off, listen to birdsong, drizzling rain, or natural sounds around you. Bring Mother Nature's presence indoors, add rocks somewhere in your home – use them as plant fillers, a door stop, or as an addition to a bathroom sink.

Open your windows wide and often, and replace recycled air with a fresh Qi.

Invite guests over and feed them this indicates you are abundant enough to feed many mouths, you generate a prosperous energy and like energy attracts more like energy. This also enhances happiness in your space.

Appreciate the true abundance in your relationships and space. When you practice appreciation in your environment, all those who come into your space feel love. When we notice and show gratitude for what is good in your life, it amplifies a trail for more success to your life.

Change your home or workspace by giving it beauty and order, and it will fill with purpose and clarity. Life imitates our environments, show and act with love daily and the big things you desire manifest more easily. When positive experiences occur around you, give thanks. This is a sign that more good things are on their way.

Keep things clean and organised.

Work together toward the same future.

When your friends or partner compliment you, thank them and let them know how happy it makes you.

Go out dancing and celebrate.

In your relationships, your task is to create harmony in your family, wherever they are.

Take enough time to enjoy people.

To have a great relationship with yourself, take a meditation class or listen to a guided meditation.

Be mindful of your boundaries. Help and mentor people but ensure you have boundaries, without them you will lose yourself in the relationship

See your partner or relationships as your greatest wealth and abundance.

Build strong bonds with your mother, loved ones and colleagues.

To avoid games and drama in your love life, avoid any kind of games, such as video games or board games, in the southwest.

Do not leave wastebaskets, clutter, or dirt in any direction that you activate.

Activate General Directions, in lounge room, workspace and bedrooms unless otherwise stated – pertaining the connected direction.

Do not place dried flowers, the positive Qi no longer exists in these.

Many have discovered the benefits of Feng Shui. If you would like to invite more success in your life with Growth and Wisdom, begin with these principles and expand the energy in your home or workspace. In the eastern culture, those who find success through Feng Shui practises do not sell their homes once they become millionaires. They keep it for luck and continued good energy, even if they move into a new house.

Everything we do is controlled by the energy we put into it. Feng Shui helps release stagnated energy and escorts in good energy. Those who find the right balance in their homes discover that when the right energy is in place their success increases. Feng Shui is an ancient science and art that many people have had success with, and it's possible for you to have that same success, as well

For complete and comprehensive balancing, activations and cures for your home or workspace, contact a Feng Shui Consultant. Please note: Direction identification with a compass is the only way to get an accurate reading of your environment. More than half of the people who conduct their own Feng Shui compass readings do it incorrectly. It's imperative that it's accurate; creating analyses based on inaccurate readings is worse than doing nothing to correct or remedy inauspicious elements in your home.

Create a Vision board

A vision board is a paper or board where you put in the centre a recent image of yourself in a enhancing outfit, depending on the type of growth or wisdom you desire, ensure the image reflects this and what it means to you. Place images around it that represent nature and natural settings in contemplation, images that make you happy, touch your feelings, of peace and learning. Place your vision board in the northeast direction in your lounge room or workspace.

Chinese Proverb

Making a thousand decisions, even the wise will make a mistake.

Be not afraid of growing slowly, be afraid only of standing still.

The Power of YOU

Your space is unique, just like you are. Learn to listen and cooperate with it. Your environment is showing you the evidence of your results as well as your thought patterns. Feng shui is there to help support your efforts, and not replace them. You are capable of anything you choose and put your mind to. You can transform your life to anything you desire. Match the frequency and you get exactly that, like attracts like. The following are statements to help you know you have the power;

Becoming wise and learned is not a matter of what environment you start in, it is a matter of causation. Things come to you when you make them come to you.

Do not accept there is no way for your growth, just remember the world as well as the universe has endless resources.

Everything we use, live in or entertain ourselves with is as a result of an initial thought, thoughts always find a way to manifest into reality. Have a clear thought of the end result. Get in the mindset of dedication and that you are a successful person and that is what you will be. It is not enough to have a general yearning for wisdom and growth, many want this, what you need it a specific goal, exactly what do you desire to attain? Exactly what do you want to be doing in one years' time? This is what you need to answer. Write with a purpose and point. It is specific aims that will come true and general aims that will not. Keep your desire in mind. Have a destination in mind, never sway from that compass and continue to move toward it. Once you have a thought live it, breath it and it will soon be a reality. The power to turn thoughts into success lies in the ability to control the way that you think. Thinking health in the midst of disease and thinking wealth in the midst of poverty is the key to success. Do not become distracted by other people's failure or they will become your own. Don't think according to what surrounds you or you have no control over your fate.

Invite growth by considering others. You should want for others what you want for yourself and growth will come to both of you.

Map your goals

Determine your personal and professional goals to ensure you align Feng Shui with your targets. Write them down and use blue ink, blue represents power. State your goals in the positive and specify what you want, not what you do not want. It must be within your control decide what you want, not what you want for another. For example, the goal "I want my husband to get a better job" is not within your control; you cannot control how someone else feels or what they want. Consider, "I help create an environment that supports my husband's success, and happiness." Ensure your goals are around what you desire. Your goal must be something you value. Not what another wants you to be, do or have. Always write your goals in the now as if they are already in place this helps stimulate the flow of Qi and the universe operates in the present moment and remember to always finish your intention with "This or something better."

Activate each goal with an image that represents your intentions, however you see this goal to be.

Being Gracious and Appreciation

Being Gracious and feeling appreciation are powerful processes, and both invite a tremendous flow of positive Qi that continues to amplify as this is practised daily. The next pages are simple lists of statements and things that help us feel good. Use these lists, choose your favourites, rewrite them, add to them, and play with them. Make this a daily occupation. Feel good now! And your abundance for health, success, relationships and growth will come swiftly.

99 Things You Can Be Gracious for on Any Given Day
I am gracious for…

1) Blazing orange and magenta sunsets
2) Quiet dawns in the darkness of early morning
3) Jacaranda trees
4) Exotic flowers like lilies and orchids
5) Books
6) Comfy, warm home on a cold day
7) Neon-green newborn grass emerging in spring
8) Supportive, loyal friends

9) Giving and receiving
10) Art in all its forms
11) Sparkles on the surface of water
12) Sturdy strong trees
13) Strong bodies that move us
14) Fairy lights
15) The first spring flower rising up
16) Optimism
17) Positivity
18) Silliness
19) Gratitude!
20) Indoor plumbing
21) Laughing till your tummy hurts
22) Deep emotion and passion
23) Our guides and angels
24) Turquoise
25) Walks in nature
26) A favorite song
27) Dancing madly
28) The golden light on nearby mountains
29) Doors for privacy
30) Quantum physics
31) Infinity
32) Worlds upon worlds

33) Feng Shui
34) A warm soup in winter
35) Clear deep rushing rivers
36) Jumpers and jackets
37) Baby lambs, puppies, kittens
38) Food glorious food
39) Too many bubbles in a bubble bath
40) My skin
41) Goofy faces
42) My happy family
43) Technology that connects the world
44) Pen and paper
45) Renoir, Picasso, Van Gogh
46) Pungent fragrances of lavender, rosemary, mint, rose
47) Pop Music to rock out to
48) Wisdom through the ages
49) Words like wonderful, luscious and nourish
50) Mother Teresa
51) Modern day mystics
52) Playtime especially when we are all grown up
53) Looking at the night sky
54) Comfortable bed
55) Unfurling of a fern frond
56) Water! Drinking it and knowing we are mostly made of it

57) The universal language of music
58) Yellow
59) Scurrying possums
60) The bustle and mix of animals, people, cars and bikes in Melbourne
61) Stretching our bodies
62) Hugs and kisses
63) Sharing with like-minded friends
64) The whole intricate, multi-layered systems of our bodies
65) Siblings through thick and thin
66) Loving, caring, nurturing mothers
67) Steady, sensible, hardworking fathers
68) Double rainbows
69) The wonder of birth!
70) Peace, quiet, serenity
71) Cars that transport us
72) The internet
73) The brilliant, bright extravaganza of summer
74) The vast ocean – the waves and tides and immensity
75) The magic of life
76) Scientists and mathematicians
77) Magenta
78) Routines we can count on
79) The fact that our world is spinning and we feel stable

80) Tropical islands
81) Dancing and laughing
82) Red
83) Melodious singers
84) The beat of drums
85) Enjoying a cool salad on a hot summer day
86) Honesty and forthrightness – people you can count on
87) Exquisite rain falling
88) Blue, and all the myriad of shades of it
89) Eyes that are a window to the soul
90) Smiles
91) Love – agape love, family love, self-love
92) The feeling of joy that upwells from within
93) The Earth's incredible beauty
94) Purple
95) Other life in the universe that is undoubtedly there
96) Particles and waves dancing and disappearing
97) Confidence and Trust
98) Kind deeds and compassion
99) All the things left off this list…

NATURAL JOYS

Think about these one at a time before going on to the next one.

1. Being in love.
2. Laughing so hard your face hurts.
3. A hot shower.
4. No queues at the supermarket.
5. Taking a drive on a pretty road.
6. Hearing your favourite song on the radio.
7. Lying in bed listening to the rain outside.
8. Hot towels fresh out of the dryer.
9. Chocolate milkshake ... or vanilla ... or strawberry!
10. A bubble bath.
11. Giggling.
12. A good conversation.
13. Finding a note in your jacket from last winter.
14. Running through sprinklers.
15. Laughing for absolutely no reason at all.
16. Having someone tell you that you're beautiful.
17. Accidentally overhearing someone say something nice about you.
18. Waking up and realising you still have a few hours left to sleep.
19. Making new friends or spending time with old ones.

20. Having someone play with your hair.

21. Sweet dreams.

22. Making eye contact with a cute stranger.

23. Holding hands with someone you care about.

24. Running into an old friend and realising that some things (good or bad) never change.

25. Watching the expression on someone's face as they open a much-desired present from you.

26. Getting out of bed every morning and being grateful for another beautiful day.

27. Knowing that somebody misses you.

28. Getting a hug from someone you care about deeply.

29. Knowing you've done the right thing, no matter what other people think.

For more information about this author
And other books:
www.terminaashton.com
www.terminafengshui.com
www.perpelflame.com
www.thehappymagnet.com

www.ingramcontent.com/pod-product-compliance
Lightning Source LLC
Chambersburg PA
CBHW050443010526
44118CB00013B/1659